Recover

Recover

Poems by Allison Joseph

Word Poetry

© 2023 by Allison Joseph

Published by Word Poetry
P.O. Box 541106
Cincinnati, OH 45254-1106

ISBN: 9781625494399

Poetry Editor: Kevin Walzer
Business Editor: Lori Jareo

Visit us on the web at www.wordpoetrybooks.com

Acknowledgements

Poems from this collection appeared previously in the following periodicals:

"Opticals": *Pirene's Fountain*

"Against Therapy": *E-Verse Radio*

"Black and White in Color": *The Raintown Review*

Contents

Recover	9
Entering Chautauqua Bottoms in Perimenopause	10
Back In the Day	12
Academic Love	14
And You Think Your Campus is Bad	16
Everest's Daughter	17
Across the Prairie	19
Administration	20
Afterglow	21
Against Therapy	22
Black and White in Color	23
Without Wings, Without Wheels	24
Somehow You Survived	25
Spell for a Neglected Poem	27
My Father, Back from the Dead, Visits to Complain About Donald Trump	28
Steady as She Goes	30
Opticals	32
About the Author	35

Recover

Doesn't matter if I stumble;
hardly matters if I fall.
I learn by learning how to fumble:

the getting up, the standing tall,
the movement back toward the light.
No matter if I'm feeling small,

my backside flat against each slight.
My gratitude's in how I play—
determination lets me write

these words. No need to stick, to stay—
escape instead familiar haunts,
old places that lead me astray.

I'm rising up against the taunts
and shaking off all flimsy
claims. I tell myself to tell it slant,

and struggle forth on shaky limbs,
take one more step, go one more mile,
hear those refrains, new sacred hymns.

No need for promises of style—
enough to make it day by day,
sustaining life through grit and guile,

persistent in my clumsy way.
Intact no matter how I crumble,
my learning comes inside the fray.

Entering Chautauqua Bottoms in Perimenopause

I wander down the street alone,
slip into this unfamiliar land—
afraid of my own invisible shadow,
regretting that I'd come this far—
away from comfy bed, warm
home of books and coffee cups.

Maybe forestry isn't for me.
Maybe I'll never be sylvan, wood nymph.
The grip I'm losing on reality
has me unsteady in these words,
these steps, admiring and fearing
enormous trees. Who told you about

my hair loss, my bleeding, my aging
unspent body? What business of that
is yours? Channeling the devil never fails
so I tramp through these muddy woods
as if I own them, these low bottoms
of washed-out paths and seasonal flood.

Hades is a town in agony
or maybe it's a space in my brain
no drug can tame, no medication.
Control yourself; stop weeping in plain sight—
I tell myself in confidence, in crisis.
Please say you'll weep with me.

Damage control eliminated me
but these woods, full of sweat and fear,
alive with the devastating winter,
might save me yet. A stick, a branch,
another risky tree ready to snap.
I stutter further, stomping these risky woods.

Back In the Day

To get to school, we'd walk
700 miles uphill in the snow,
our shoes held together by rubber
cement and paper clips, blizzards

smacking us in the backs of our
heads if we tried to protest
in our grocery bag dresses
and our prison uniform slacks.

Back then, we had no smart
phones, no phones at all, really—
we communicated through
tin can relays and passenger

pigeon notes, foot messengers,
and, if really lucky, out of work
angels. We didn't have clocks
or watches or anything

digital—except our fingers,
which we used to keep track
of everything—how many kids
in each family, how many

measles on each kid, how many
chicken pox. And speaking of
chicken, chicken were giant hairy
enormous beasts, and every day we would

pray that our giant chicken
overlords would not kill us
in our sleep, wring our necks
for their pleasure. As for

pleasure, we didn't have
YouTube or Snapchat, no—
no internet or videogames—
we drew in the dirt with

sticks, smeared our faces
with mud, and ran around
shirtless—boys and girls
both—all dirty muscles

and talons, ice cream dripping from
our filthy fingers, greedy mouths.
Yes, of course, we had ice cream!
What do you think we were, uncivilized?

Academic Love

Let's write each other's references
and blurb each other's blurbs
I look at you with reverence
consuming all your words

Let's cite each other's monographs
and quote each other's work
Let's sigh and give a rueful laugh
at all our classroom quirks

Let's be each other's proxy vote
while everybody frowns
We'll turn a do into a don't
and shut our colleagues down

Let's form our own official force
avoiding all those tasks
and chart an independent course
no audits if they ask

Let's make committee work a dance
that's only meant for two
A shuttered office door at last
for our program review

Let's let our subjects write themselves
engrossed in our smart minds
and write more books for laden shelves
that academic grind

But let's not stay until we die
and wither from the strain
of knowing that it's all a lie
these academic gains

Let's tear away our caps and gowns
one graduation day
in gladness that we're still around
alive despite the gray

And You Think Your Campus is Bad

University of the Fake Seminar.
Pipebomb U. College of the Immaculate
Deception, all transfers from Our Lady

of Loose Morals Junior College
gleefully accepted. Rotting Infrastructure
Institute—engineering the most popular major.

Failure Academy, which, of course,
is entirely online. College of the Clogged Artery,
where one can major only in nutritional science.

Hair Clog U. University of the Severed
Right Thigh, with multiple campuses up
and down the Eastern seaboard. Salmonella

Institute, specializing in culinary arts. Earn your
bachelor's in Bacterial Studies there. Camel Toe
College of Interior and Fashion Design. University

of the Sucker Punch, of the Crotch Kick,
of the Eternal Panty Raid. Broken Molar U,
School of Excruciating Dentistry.

And lastly, every little girl's dream
school: Anorexia Nervosa College
of the Military and Liberal Arts.

Everest's Daughter

At least I didn't have a name
as weighty and foreboding as
my father's, who was named
not just for a mountain but for

the highest peak on earth.
I have the name of a good
girl, a nice woman, well-
behaved lady who will not

raise her voice despite how
much you test her with lies
and excuses, half-truths
and bigotry. I have the name

of your middle daughter,
quiet one who would never
sneak out in midnight dark
to meet some boy in back

of his father's rusty sedan.
Unlike my father, I have no
heights to live up to, no
treacherous ascents, nothing

to climb and nowhere to
cling to by a fingerhold,
no peril except from the
memories of him growling

my name in his rages,
his anger so unsettling
I'd jump at the thud
of his footsteps on the stairs,

at the snap of his belt.
Perhaps I hadn't been
such a good girl after all,
and however I'd set off

his daily fury, I knew he'd
call me out of my plain name,
heating up each syllable until
my ears rang, and I cried

as silently as I could,
not daring utter any
of the names I'd call him:
Daddy, father, hero, joke.

Across the Prairie

Should you be satisfied with this terrain
of clapboard houses, fallow wizened fields—
the landscape brushing past you on this train?
Should you sit here content with what it yields:
those brittle stalks of corn so far from silk,
those shiny silver silos beckoning,
small-town cafés dispensing coldest milk,
thick slabs of apple pie? You're reckoning
there's nothing here for you among these towns
this train will barrel through without a stop—
no counter job, no store, no wedding gown,
no city hall where you're the only cop.
But who can say your future can't be found
among this plain's stark trees, raw autumn ground?

Administration

The world is full of shady liars,
so gleefully they ply their trade!
I'll dance around their funeral pyres.

We run around, put out their fires,
aggrieved while they sip lemonade.
The world is full of shady liars

who barely do what life requires—
they make each one of us their maid.
I'll dance around their funeral pyres,

sing happy hymns when they expire.
Is this the end for which I've prayed?
The world is full of shady liars

who smile at you, then slash your tires,
destroying floats at your parade.
I'll dance around their funeral pyres

and giggle as the flames grow higher,
set free at last from all charades.
The world is full of shady liars—
so dance, around and around, those cleansing fires!

Afterglow

Let love lie languidly upon your lips,
a taste of skin and sweat, of vibrant heat
you shouldn't wipe away with fingertips
rinsed clean of it. You need not be discreet
and wash all evidence of touch away,
eliminating how you tangled here—
the tossed and grizzled sheets where you both lay,
abandoned skirts or pants. Don't rush to clear
the mess your joining bought, the disarray
of nudity and breath, of thighs and backs
against the fitted sheet, mattress astray.
Leave it askew, undone, your lives gone slack.
The looser that your limbs become the more
you know this languid life's worth living for.

Against Therapy

It's easier to write than sit and gawk
at someone paid to listen to me whine,
a therapist who only gives her time
as long as I can pay without a squawk,
show up on time and never seem to balk
at anything she claims will fix my mind,
that fertile place she'd like to bring in line
with everybody else's doubletalk.
I'd rather be alone with this blank page
than gaze into her kind of caring face,
than stare at all her books, her framed degrees.
This page won't try to pacify my rage,
or numb my grief with promises of grace
if I could only live the life she sees.

Black and White in Color

In bed, I watch in woozy misery.
Home sick from work, I'm watching trashy shows
where people revel in their histories
of so-called marriages, cheaters brought low
by catcalls from the audience. The host,
avuncular and rich, tries to allay
the tears of these young girls whose partners boast
of infidelities like kids at play
which is, of course, still what these couples are.
My head's so clogged, but not so clogged I can't
hear every accusation hurled, the scars
unfolding on daytime TV, the want.
I try to turn it off, but I'm held back:
why must so much dysfunction come in black?

Without Wings, Without Wheels

I walk to get the rhythms out
to work the ground beneath my feet
to stumble shuffle roam and stop
to catch the tears before I weep

I walk to keep the fears at bay
that rising tide of ugliness
that turns me up against myself
I build myself back up again

I walk to keep my name intact
those syllables upon my tongue—
remind myself of where I fell
and how the dust felt on my palms

I walk to free myself of doubt
to feel my breath in shivering
in love with just my threadbare coat
and a portion of the sea

I walk in sand, in moss and muck,
in grace and in my clumsiness
in gratitude and willingness
to rise when landscape asks me too—

the lights ahead and town below
I walk to hear those rhythms build
I walk and let them all subside:
a wave, a wave, a blesséd wave.

Somehow You Survived

for Dennis Brutus, in memory of his 1995 visit to
Carbondale, Illinois

Somehow you survived
the legacy of a shameful nation
that did not see your glory—

its anthems not for you,
for "coloured" you in exile,
one way ticket out of your homeland,

territory you cherished though it
shot you down, let you bleed on
the street in Johannesburg, dragged

you to trial, shipped you to a cell,
imprisoned you in the rocky cruelty
of Robben Island, Mandela one cell

over. Somehow your tenderness,
your humor, your tenacity
survived in the wake of presidents

and politics, sport and the desperate
beauty of cities held hostage by global
forces—boots on the ground, secret

police and Secret Service, dictators
and demagogues. I heard you speak
of hope in the face of death,

of love in the midst of anger,
of home in the midst of exile.
I heard you speak with the tenderness

of a man outliving his captors,
his jailers, poet set on wandering
wherever tenderness lets him imagine,

surrendering over and over
that peculiar sudden hope,
that simple lust in life.

Spell for a Neglected Poem

I resurrect this poem from the dead,
brush off the faulty lines and set them right,
remind myself that they came from my head,
remember I abandoned them that night,

forgot them in the glare of morning light,
went onto to write some other piece instead,
some easy passage much less prone to fight.
I resurrect this poem from the dead,

unwind it bit by bit, and thread by thread,
to turn it into something I could write
with joy and not a creeping sense of dread.
Brush off the faulty lines and set them right,

fill in the gaps and joints, my rhythms tight.
I plot and scratch, step back, my papers spread
across the floor. I free these lines from spite,
remind myself that they came from my head,

investigating work I could have shred,
its newer possibilities in sight,
my words revealing how lived and fled.
Remember I abandoned them that night?
I resurrect this poem.

My Father, Back from the Dead, Visits to Complain About Donald Trump

He's looking really sharp for a dead guy,
but then again, my father always could dress well—
leather shoes, pressed suits, cufflinks and tie pins,

because my father always knew he couldn't
get away with being slovenly, that he couldn't
be angry with anyone but us, in his

home, his own falling-apart castle.
I tell him that it's been like this for what seems
like years, and that black people, who are

usually merely just fed-up with all the hypocrisy
and indignities, need him back fiercely.
Only you can make me feel better,

I say, forgiving him those rages in my girlhood
violent moody swings of temper that left me
loving him and hating him in the same day.

How can you trust a white man that orange,
my father sneers, and I feel a wash of relief—
this time, my father's scathing sarcasm is

headed for Trump Tower, to DC—where
he took us once on a rare family vacation,
occasion of one of my few photos with him.

My father says *white people don't come in
tangerine* and I roar aloud, tears coming
into my eyes with love for his snark,

for his petty meanness now thrust at
the Starburst-In-Chief, for my father remembers
I loved that candy, particularly the orange ones,

wrappers all over my childhood bedroom,
decorating my hand-me-down dresser.
My father's ghost demands: *you mean to tell*

me that's the best this country could do
after all this time I've been away?
He never felt a need to visit during the Obama

years—though I'm sure he would have poked
fun at Barack too—those ears too much
to resist. But this, this orange clown, this real

estate loser, this reality show ringmaster—
he's enough to raise an angry black man
spitting and yelling and reeling from

the dead, my father's loud Caribbean timbre
waking me from my abject American sleep,
my green card slumber, my citizenship
not the only gift this father ever gave me.

Steady as She Goes

You're calling me unstable
        but shaking is my strength
I tremble but I'm able
        to go to any length

to do what I require
        to shimmy in my strut
a streak of rage inspired
        by every wound and cut

No kit of matching pieces
        no parts to fit your slots
I'm finding what my reach is
        I run both cold and hot

Let colors flare obnoxious
        let freaky flags commence
I'm tired of feeling toxic
        I want uncommon sense

I live to thrum and flutter
        to rise and crash and soar
defendant in my clutter
        unique in my allure

Check me—a thrift store bargain—
        effective but quite cheap
You know you find me charming
        that dream you crave in sleep

Let fury flare defiant
        let laughter hiss from me
such boredom in compliance
        with what we're supposed to be

And if you try to dim me
        you'll suffer in my light
No point to living grimly
        when I serve this delight

Opticals

Without them I stumble to see, two fogged
windowpanes over my lids, hooks on each end
to latch them over my ears, tiny translucent pads
that sit on the bridge of my nose, the whole contraption
 held together by screws so tiny I couldn't see them
if they fell to the floor, lodged in the carpet.
"Made in Japan" is printed on one earpiece
in white lettering so minute it looks as if the tiniest
brush in the world must have made the JAPAN.
So much more flexible than I am, and without them
everything looks worse: words blurry around edges,
but with them I can see my own flaws better, whether
or not I want to—these lenses make every pore
visible. They own their own house, case
that opens and shut with a click, protects them
while I sleep, keeping safe their skinny little hinges,
the wire frames around their smudged ovals,
my thumbprints manic all over their surfaces.
If I sat on them, they'd break. The woman's voice
 on my answering machine says it's time to see
the eye doctor again. I ignore her and squint at
the fine print on my bills. One scratch and they
are useless. My husband takes them off my face
and swears, *how do you see out of these things?*
They grow oily from the touch of my fingers—
after years of declining eyesight I still check
to see if they are there. In sunlight, their lenses
turn black so my corneas don't get scorched,
so I look like a cop from a 70's TV show or an
alien with sockets for eyes. Note to self: avoid
sunlight. I'll wear them to the movies, but not in photos.

I finally found this pair that fits across the bridge
of my broad nose without those dastardly red
marks, but the right earpiece fits more snugly

which makes me think my ears are deformed,
or the optician had no idea was she was doing.
But I wear them, perched precarious and silly,
push them back onto my nose all day long.
At night, I slip them back into their smooth velvet house.
Night's the only time I don't need them
because I don't see anything in focus as I dream.

About the Author

Allison Joseph lives, teaches, and writes in Carbondale, Illinois, where she is part of the creative writing faculty at Southern Illinois University Carbondale. Her previous collections of poetry include *Lexicon* (Red Hen Press, winner of the Poetry by the Sea Best Book Award), *Confessions of a Barefaced Woman* (Red Hen Press, winner of the Feathered Quill Book Award and finalist for the NAACP Image Award in Poetry), and the chapbooks *Speak and Spell* (Glass Lyre Press) and *Any Proper Weave* (Kelsay Books). She is the widow of beloved late poet and editor Jon Tribble.

Made in the USA
Columbia, SC
10 February 2024

31211167R00024